Daddy's Heroes®

Unforgettable Sports Moments To Share With Children

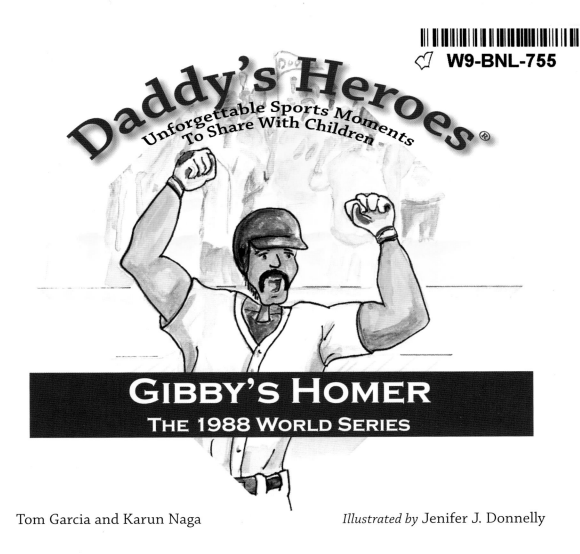

GIBBY'S HOMER
THE 1988 WORLD SERIES

Tom Garcia and Karun Naga

Illustrated by Jenifer J. Donnelly

ISBN 978-0-9792111-0-2

All rights reserved. Published by Daddy's Heroes, Inc.
Printed in Hong Kong.

It was a chilly October evening in the City of Los Angeles.

Lots of boys and girls and moms and dads filled Dodger Stadium to cheer for the **Los Angeles Dodgers** as they played the **Oakland A's**.

It was the first game of the World Series. The first team to win four games would be the champions.

Nobody knew that this would be one of the best baseball games ever!

The boys and girls found their seats in the big stadium. Some bought peanuts, hot dogs and souvenirs.

Everybody was so excited for the game.

But would their favorite Dodgers beat the A's?

The A's were the strongest team in baseball.

Nobody thought the Dodgers could win.

The A's powerful hitting was led by the dangerous Bash Brothers —

Muscle-Bound Mark
and
Heavy-Hitting Jose.

The A's also had the best pitcher in all of baseball — *Awesome Eck*.

Everybody knew that when Eck entered the game, it was game over for the other team.

The A's were a great baseball team!

The Dodgers also had many star players, but their clever coach, *Tommy*, was the heart and soul of the team.

Tommy loved to eat Italian food, especially pasta.

The only thing Tommy loved more than pasta was his Dodgers.

Gibby the Great was the best player of all the Dodgers.

He was a "clutch" hitter who always seemed to get the big hit.

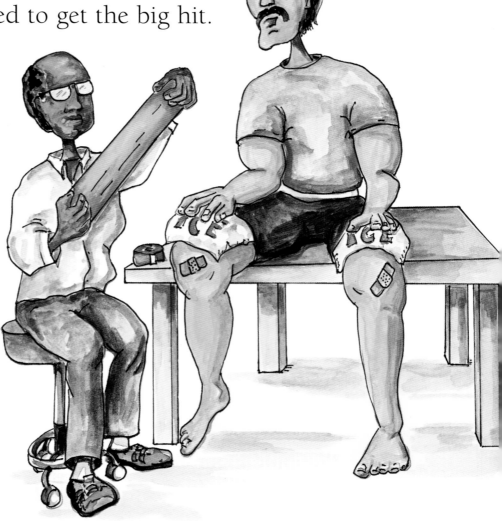

Everybody loved Gibby,
but his legs were hurt,
and he could barely walk.

Nobody thought that
Gibby would play.

*How could the Dodgers
beat the A's without Gibby
that day?*

The Dodgers took the field and the crowd roared with excitement.

Gibby stayed in the clubhouse to care for his injuries.

The Dodgers were winning the game and loved hearing the loud cheers from the fans!

The A's came back in the next inning and quickly loaded the bases.

Who was batting next?

Heavy-Hitting Jose!

"Oh, no!"

Jose blasted a homerun to center field for a grand slam! Oh what a shame for the Dodgers!!

With one swing of Jose's bat, the A's were now winning the game.

The A's kept their lead throughout the game.

Everyone knew that if the A's held their lead, Eck would come into the game.

The boys and girls started to worry when they saw Awesome Eck practicing in the bullpen.

It was the last inning.

"Oh no!" Awesome Eck entered the game to pitch for the A's.

Did this mean "game over" for the Dodgers? Eck only needed outs one, two and three.

He easily got one and two and the A's started to celebrate.

The Dodger fans had lost all hope.

But then, to everyone's surprise, Eck walked the next hitter.

"Hooray!"

Coach Tommy had a great idea.

Tommy was checking on Gibby all game long, and now . . . Gibby was feeling good enough to go to bat.

When Gibby stepped onto the field with his big baseball bat, the crowd went crazy.

Everyone knew that a homerun would win the game for the Dodgers.

But when Gibby limped to the batter's box, the crowd knew that Gibby was hurt.

Gibby was having trouble with Eck's super-fast pitches.

Everyone thought that Gibby was just too hurt to hit the ball.

Gibby was just waiting for the best pitch.

Then came the last pitch — Gibby was ready! Eck threw the ball, Gibby swung with all his might.

Gibby hit the ball very, very far. . .

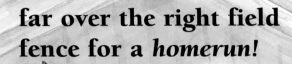

far over the right field fence for a *homerun!*

As Gibby limped around the bases, the Dodgers and their fans cheered and cheered and **cheered**!

The Dodgers won the game! And they won the World Series that year.

*T*he Dodgers' road to the championship began during the regular season where they amassed an impressive record of 94 wins and 67 losses. The pitching staff dominated the National League with Orel Hershiser leading the way. Orel finished his Cy Young Award season with a 23-8 record, including a record 59 consecutive scoreless innings to end the season. Although Kirk Gibson was injured much of the season, his intensity, leadership and clutch hitting earned him the National League Most Valuable Player award.

The A's dominated the American League with a record of 104 wins and 58 losses. Their talented lineup was led by Jose Canseco, the American League Most Valuable Player, who in 1988 became the first player to hit 40 home runs and steal 40 bases in the same season. Dave Stewart was the ace of the pitching staff and the team's closer, Dennis Eckersley, saved a league-leading 45 games. No one was surprised when the A's swept the Boston Red Sox in the American League Championship Series by winning four consecutive games.

While the A's had an easy time with the Red Sox, the Dodgers were pushed to the brink of elimination by the New York Mets in the National League Championship Series. The superb play of Kirk Gibson and Orel Hershiser gave the Dodgers the edge as they beat the Mets in a tough-fought, seven game series (4-3). Gibson hit a game-winning home run in Game 4 of the series. Orel was named the Series MVP after throwing a complete-game shutout in the deciding Game 7.

Gibson and Hershiser continued their leadership in the World Series, with Gibson winning Game 1 for the Dodgers in his sole at bat of the Series. Following Gibson's inspirational performance, Hershiser dominated with complete game wins in Games 2 and 5 to earn the World Series MVP Award. Mark McGwire's game-winning home run in Game 3 helped the A's avoid a sweep, but there was nothing that the A's could do to deny the Dodgers the Championship. They were a team of destiny.